Watching Comets

T0351222

Written by Jo Windsor

Contents

What are comets?

Comets are clumps of ice, rock and dust that fly through space. They look like bright balls with a hazy patch that stretches out behind them. Comets are also called 'dirty snowballs'!

Comets are part of our **solar system**. They follow orbits, or circular paths, through space as they travel around the Sun. Because of their orbits, they come back from time to time. Sometimes, we can see comets from Earth.

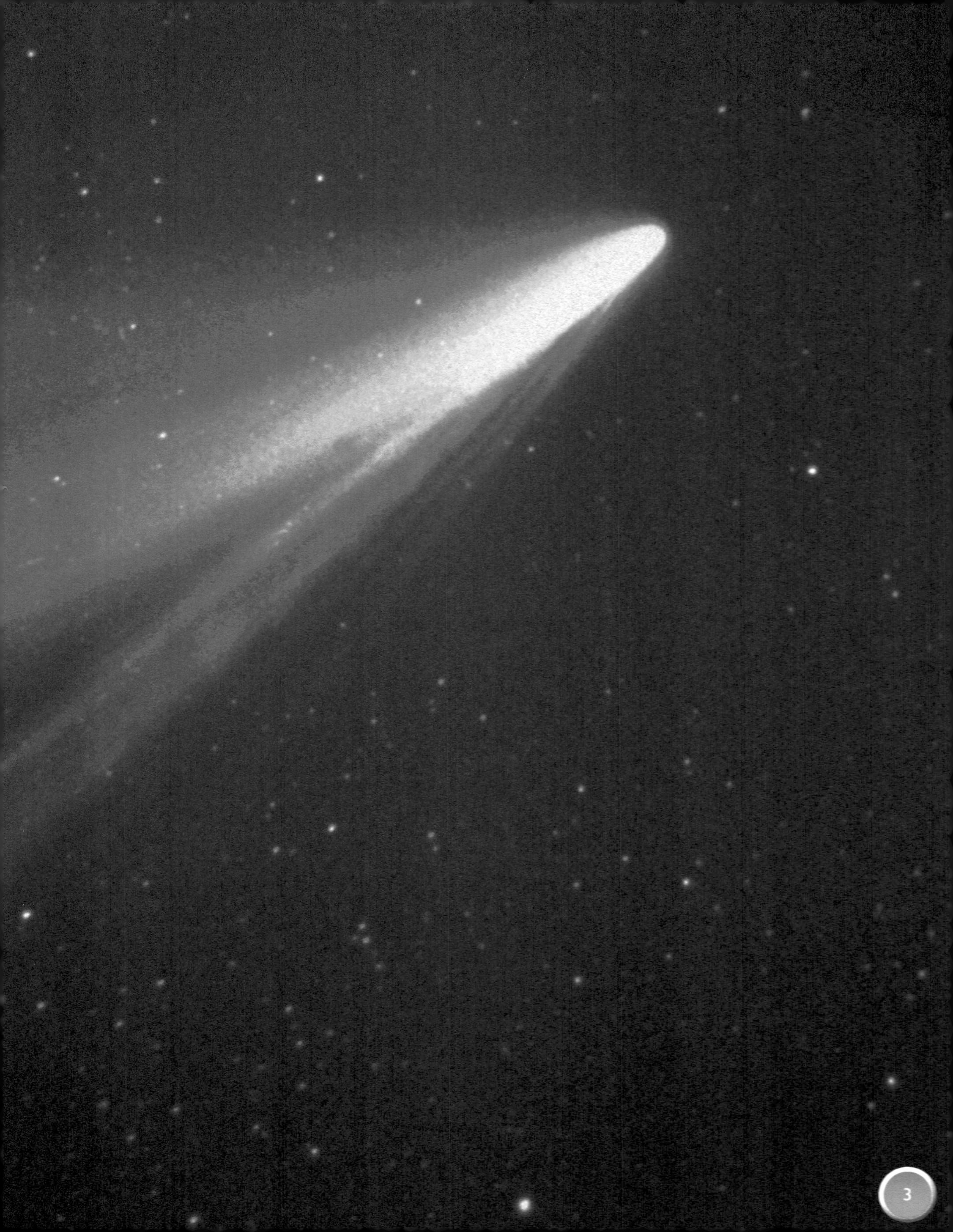

Heads and tails

Comets come in a variety of sizes and shapes. They have a head and they have tails. The icy head can be big or small. When a comet travels close to the Sun, it begins to light up. It starts to melt and, as the gases in the head get hot, it begins to glow. The head of the comet gets brighter.

Most comets have two tails. One tail consists of gas and the other, dust. The tails begin to grow longer and they look brighter as the comet moves along. The tails can be thousands of kilometres long.

In the past, people thought a comet looked like a woman's head with long hair flowing out behind it. The word comet comes from the Greek word *coma*, meaning hair.

gas tail

dust tail

head

Travelling through space

On the very edge of the solar system are two areas called the Oort Cloud and the Kuiper Belt. Here, millions of comets have swirled around for billions of years.

Some comets travel into the solar system, around the Sun, and out again. They travel in circular orbits. They can appear and disappear anywhere in the sky and, if they **collide**, they can move away in any direction.

A comet leaves a trail of dust behind it as it travels. When Earth moves into this dust we see **shooting stars** in the sky.

As a comet travels through space, the gas tail always points away from the Sun. So, the gas tail is in front of the head as it travels away from the Sun.

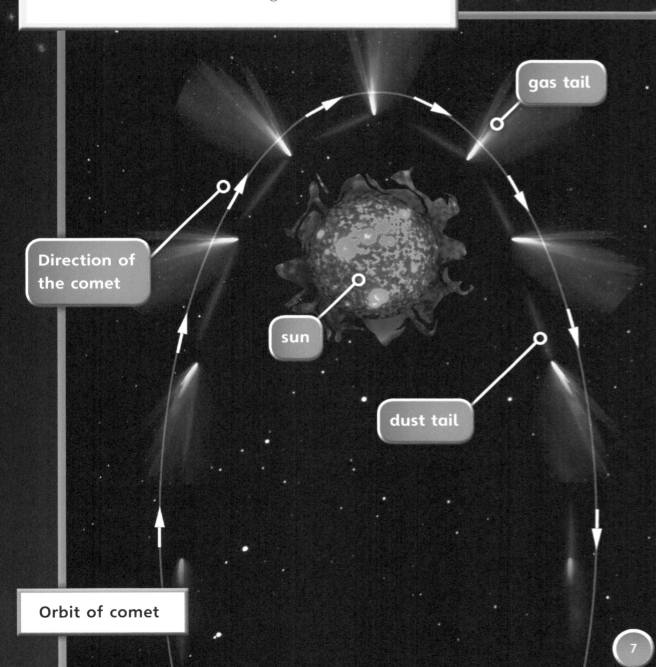

gas tail

Direction of the comet

sun

dust tail

Orbit of comet

An omen

People who lived long ago knew very little about their world. When comets suddenly appeared without warning in the sky, many people were frightened of them. They believed comets were an **omen** that would bring bad luck. They would pray and ring church bells. Many people also thought that the tail of a comet would hit Earth and destroy it.

The Great Comet of 1811

Death of a comet

Every time a comet travels around the Sun, some of its icy material starts to **evaporate**, forming the tail. Over thousands of years, the comet gets smaller and smaller and eventually the icy parts are gone.

A comet colliding with the planet Jupiter

2

comet

1

moon

Jupiter

4

crater

3

impact

The **core** that remains may be quite small.
If the core contains no rocks, the comet just
disappears altogether and leaves nothing but
a cloud of dust. The comet dies.

Sometimes, a comet will die by colliding with
the Sun or a planet.

Tracking a famous comet

A long time ago, a brilliant comet blazed in Earth's skies. Many people watched it, but it was Edmund Halley, an **astronomer**, who **predicted** it would return. The comet did return and it became known as Halley's Comet. It will return again in 2061.

Edmund Halley

Halley's Comet photographed from California in the USA in 1986

Throughout history, Halley's Comet has been sighted many times. Each time, information about the sighting has been recorded.

Timeline of Halley's Comet

Year 240 BC

The first recorded sighting of the comet that would later become known as Halley's Comet.

Year	300 BC	200 BC	100 BC

The Chinese made sketches of comets as far back as 186 BC. They called comets 'broom stars', thinking that the tails looked like the bristles of a broom.

The Chinese also called comets 'vile stars'. They, too, thought the sighting of a comet could bring disasters such as floods, drought, disease or even the death of their Emperor.

Year AD 141

Halley's Comet was mentioned in Chinese records.

Year 163 BC

A sighting of Halley's Comet was recorded on a clay tablet discovered in 1985.

AD 100   AD 200   AD 300

Year AD 66

Halley's Comet was mentioned in Chinese records. The people of this time believed that the Comet would bring destruction.

A woodcut showing Halley's Comet, made in AD 684

Year AD 684

The oldest known picture of Halley's Comet is on a **woodcut**. People who saw it predicted catastrophic storms, a poor harvest and a **plague**.

Year   AD 400   AD 600   AD 800

Year AD 837

Halley's Comet was mentioned in Chinese records. This was the best sighting so far. The comet came within eight million kilometres of Earth.

ISTI MIRANT STELLA

comet

HAROLD

Year AD 1066

This famous French tapestry is called *The Bayeux Tapestry*. One part of it shows a comet. It is thought to be Halley's Comet.

AD 1000   AD 1200   AD 1400 ▶

1300s

An Italian artist called Giotto painted a picture of the Three Wise Men at Bethlehem. In the background, we see Halley's Comet moving across the night sky.

Giotto's painting The Three Wise Men at Bethlehem

Year AD 1682

The comet was first observed by Halley. He used information about **prior** sightings and his scientific knowledge to predict that the comet would return.

Year   **AD 1650**   **AD 1700**   **AD 1750**

Watching Halley's Comet in 1759

Year AD 1759

Halley's Comet returned. It returned one year later than Halley predicted because it had passed close to the planet of Jupiter. Jupiter has a strong gravitational pull that slowed the comet down.

Year AD 1835

For the first time, ordinary people were able to enjoy watching the comet. The people of that time had begun to have a greater understanding about what a comet was and their fear was replaced by curiosity.

Watching Halley's Comet in 1835

AD 1800   AD 1850   AD 1900

A painting based on photos taken in California in 1910

Year AD 1910

Scientists observed Halley's Comet as it crossed the sky. Even so, there were still many people who feared that the comet's appearance was a warning about disaster. People bought 'comet pills', gas masks and umbrellas to protect themselves from the 'evil' that the comet would bring, but nothing happened!

Year AD 1986

The return visit of Halley's Comet was disappointing as it was only just visible in many parts of the world.

The comet was at its brightest when it was furthest away from Earth, so by the time it reached Earth it was very faint. People studied it closely through telescopes.

A **space probe**, *Giotto*, was sent up into space to take pictures of the comet and send them back to Earth. After an eight-month journey across the solar system, *Giotto* flew within 600 kilometres of the comet. This gave us the first close-up view of a comet. Scientists have used the pictures to help them understand more about comets.

Year   **AD 1950**   **AD 2000**

Halley's Comet seen above the giant stone statues on Easter Island in the Pacific Ocean in March 1986

The Giotto space probe travelled close to Halley's Comet in 1986

Year AD 2061

Halley's Comet will return again.

AD 2050

Stamps were issued all over the world to commemorate the 1986 sighting of Halley's Comet

REPUBLIQUE DE DJIBOUTI

POSTES 1986

USTI MIRANT STELLA

Passage de la Comète de HALLEY

85 F

EDILA

VERET LEMARINIER

Catching comet dust

Comets provide information about the origins of Earth. In February 1999, the *Stardust* spacecraft was launched from its base in the USA on a twelve-year **mission** to space. Its job was to catch comet dust and return it to Earth so that scientists could study it.

The launch of *Stardust* from Kennedy Space Center, USA

The material *Stardust* collected is very important to our understanding of planets, and to planning future missions to space.

Stardust completed its mission in March 2011.

The *Stardust* probe

The *Stardust* capsule returning to Earth with comet dust

A space mission

To understand more about comets, a mission to land a spacecraft on a comet is part of a long-term space programme. A spacecraft called the *Rosetta* was launched in 2004 on an eleven-year mission to meet 'Comet 46'. It carries a small probe called a lander. The lander is collecting information about the comet and its environment.

An artist's impression of the *Rosetta*, its lander, and a comet

The *Rosetta* swooping over the lander just after its touchdown on a comet

The information collected is sent back to Earth via a radio link. Engineers and scientists have a challenging job to land this craft successfully. They may have to deal with the comet's fragile surface, a difficult landscape and extremes of temperature. If this mission is successful, it will give scientists many clues about our Sun and its planets.

Did comets kill the dinosaurs?

This is the big question, and different people have different opinions. Scientists do seem to agree on some theories:

1 There is **evidence** that the climate changed dramatically all over the world 65 million years ago.

2 Much of Earth's surface was disturbed. Soot and dust were thrown into the air, making **acid rain** and poisonous gases, and cooling down temperatures.

3 Dinosaurs and other life-forms became **extinct** as a result.

Did comets cause the dramatic **global** climate change and kill the dinosaurs? No one really knows.

Make comet balls!

What you need

- some polystyrene balls, about 4cm in diameter
- glue
- glitter
- 2 small bowls to hold the glue and glitter
- some pins
- 4 metallic coloured ribbons for each ball
- pipe cleaner
- brush to use with the glue

What you do:

1 Cut a piece of the pipe cleaner – about a quarter of its length.

2 Line up the ends of the four ribbons and hold together with a pin.

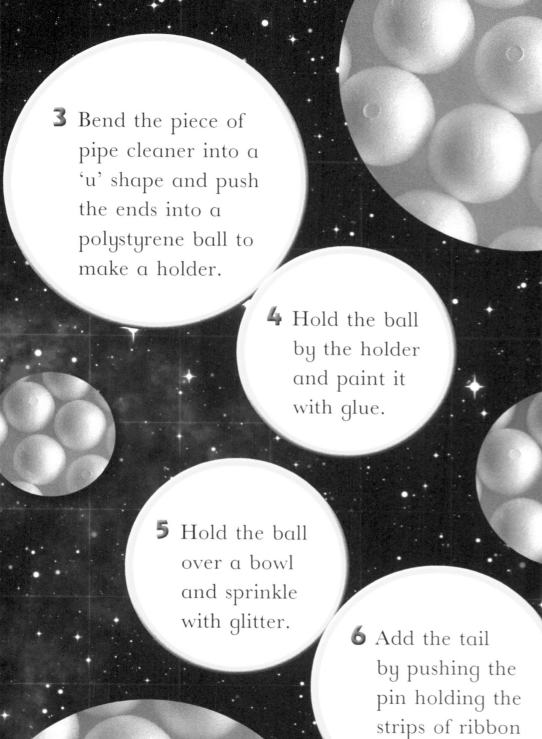

3 Bend the piece of pipe cleaner into a 'u' shape and push the ends into a polystyrene ball to make a holder.

4 Hold the ball by the holder and paint it with glue.

5 Hold the ball over a bowl and sprinkle with glitter.

6 Add the tail by pushing the pin holding the strips of ribbon into the ball.

Quiz

1 What do comets consist of?
   a snow, mud and gravel
   b ice, rock and dust
   c metal, rubber and plastic

2 What else are comets known as?
   a dirty ice balls
   b dirty rock balls
   c dirty snowballs

3 What do comets travel around?
   a the Sun
   b the Moon
   c Earth

4 What do we see in the trail of a comet's dust?
   a a rainbow
   b a fire
   c shooting stars

Answers on page 31

Glossary

acid rain   acid that falls in rain, hail, sleet and snow

astronomer   scientist who studies stars and planets

collide   crash into

core   central part

evaporate   turn from solid into vapour

evidence   something that helps to form an opinion

extinct   no longer living

global   over the whole world

mission   group of experts sent to explore something

omen   good or bad sign

plague   disease or pest that spreads quickly

predicted   told about before it happened

prior   something that has gone before

shooting stars bright streaks of light seen falling in the sky at night

solar system   Sun and every planet, moon and comet that moves around it

space probe   spacecraft with scientific instruments that records data in space

woodcut   image carved onto piece of wood from which a print can be taken

Quiz answers: 1b; 2c; 3a; 4c

Index